Golden Palm Trees

by Paulette Lewis-Brown

authorHOUSE®

AuthorHouse™
1663 Liberty Drive
Bloomington, IN 47403
www.authorhouse.com
Phone: 1 (800) 839-8640

Published by AuthorHouse 03/06/2018

ISBN: 978-1-5462-3166-0 (sc)
ISBN: 978-1-5462-3165-3 (e)

Print information available on the last page.

Contents

Palm Tree Delight

Send in the fun time
Send in the plate to unwind
Send in the Nature Tree high
it's a Cup cake for you and I.

Palm Tree Delight
Beautiful day
Everyone looks fine.
Smile with the Nature
In me. You are the moment
So feel free.

Gold and Green
Pick a color from
The Rainbow.
Wave your fingers
for a cool flow.

Enjoy the Sun light
Keep every thoughts
Close. Love is everything
So don't brag or boast.
No more fight, it's time to
Eat your Palm Tree Delight.

This's your first Poetry Treat
Palm Tree Delight.
The Sugar is free.
Compliment from Golden
Palm Tree.

Celebrate Each other Success

Oh what a beauty
Everyone is stepping
Out in style.
All road leads to the
Vintage and Antique
Gloves for awhile.
Everyone is different
Your story could fit in
A shoe. Enjoy the Queen
And Princesses in you. Enjoy the
Sportsman that didn't finish
College. Here comes the
Photographer, say cheese.
Stay on Par, here comes the
Doctor, Nurses and Gym Master.
Everyone is smiling when they saw
Their Teacher. Life is fun with a test.
When we celebrate each other Success.
We always strive to be our best.

Be The Creative One

Think outside the box
Draw from the Energy
Around you.
Feed from a safety Net.
Bring out the colors in you
Be different, that's cool.
Golden Palm Tree is your
Luxury base. Please don't
leave the Sun behind.
I really want to see green
All over your thoughts. Mix
Everything together, like your'e
Baking a Cake. Your masterpiece
is to be Creative, make it Rain.
This's A plan, your goal is to be
The Creative one, no one saw coming.
A touch of Gold for the Win.

Palm Tree Money

Money for every Palm Tree insight.
This's Alzheimer's Charity fight.
Welcome everything that comes with
This Challenge. Someday we will all
Have Wings for balance.
Money is just for the moment
Our Awareness will live on forever.
Our love will last for a lifetime
Caring one for another.
No need to cry my dear Love.
Palm Tree Money is a blessing.
Take it on every Walk. Smile when
You see a white Dove. Wave and
Say Palm Tree Money Honey.

Where is the Sun

Where is the Sun to Balance
My Sun down moment.
Where is the Nature Tree that
Remembers my Anniversary.
Where is the Red Wine or Apple
Cider. Where is my Aide to feed
Me my super. Where is my Family
To invite me over. Where is my best
Friend Trevor. Where is the Sun to
guide my footsteps. Where is the Vitamin D
Before I wear my new dress. Where is my
Furry friend Rex. Where is my Makeup to
blend with my Jewelry. Where is my
Mindset to balance my mood.
Where is the Sun to follow me for my daily run.
Please Lord where is the Sun. I need more fun.

Beautiful Roses

Everything you touch looks beautiful
Everywhere you travel sends off a spark.
Everyone you meet smile from ear to ear
Beautiful Rose open wide, with birthday
Anniversaries by her side.
Sharing and spreading real love.
Red Roses are visible everywhere.
Embrace this white calm Dove.
Count in the moment of silence.
Every Rose in this group is a beautiful bunch.
Beautiful,beautiful Roses, put them together
for this phase. out of nowhere came this
Crystal Vase. Beautiful Red Rose for everyone.

I Live My Life

I Dream of a very good life.
I live a very challenged one
I give to every spur of the moment
I share to be redeemed from the Sun
I survive every Hurricane
I float in every Storm
I embrace Faith, Family and Friends
That's the norm.
I live my life gracefully until the end.
Now this's your moment to live your
Life over again, wake up and enjoy your passion.
Never a dull moment from this day on.
Find your Inner strength to carry on.

Nature at it's Best

Explore the World with Nature beside you.
Enjoy the Ocean search for the clue
Elope with the one that you love
Smile with the Haters, find time to love real
Nature. Wrap your Heart around Mr Blue sky.
Remember that everyday is a test, fly high.
Passing is easy when you spread your Wings
First, then enjoy Nature at its best.
Watch the Trees waving in the Wind.
Birds flying in the Rain, get that rhythm
Nature at it's and you by his side.
Reveal your picture of love, last note filled with
Flowers.
Nature at it's best is a work of Art.

Drop the Scale

Finally we can eat our cake in Peace
Enjoying a glass of Red Wine when we
Eat. Dancing in your White dress with no
Limits. Remembering the good times
No more blues. Everyone is a winner
No need to fail. know that your'e beautiful
So go ahead and drop the scale.
Weight is now everyone ball game.
Sock it to me in the Hall of fame. Call me
The yellow Bird with a green Tail, black is
Beautiful, so is the whale.
Smile when you can tell me which two Countries
Drop the scale. Moonwalk for this one. Check your
Pulse then drop the scale.

Glitter my Mood

Sprinkle some glitter on my mood
I just want to feel strong and smooth
No hitch on my Tail
No glitch on my Frail
Sprinkle some Glitter on my Mood.
Don't leave me too soon.
Cry me a river could send me to the Moon
Glitter my mood with some chicken Soup.
Send me a world wind to humble my Soul
Give me a promise to have and to hold.
Glitter my Mood, even if you cannot see me.
Happy, Happy Joy, Joy sprinkle some free.
Glitter on my Mood. Shine for the world to read.

Glass House Poetry

I can read through your thoughts
Attach this note to a Calvary of Mountain
Send me a life time of memories
Seal my Faith, give me room to breathe
I can see herd of troubles waving, give me
A no mans land to lay my head. Walk with me
Save the day ahead of tomorrow. I can see no
more today, so I will jump to the future.
Glass House Poetry could see things that way.
Open your mind, with a beautiful Rainbow
Plug me in, Free the socket to recharge my battery.
Why is everyone looking at me. No I am not crazy.
Leave room in your Heart and welcome Glass House
Poetry. Don't throw any stones. Hope is outside waiting
For a new start. This's one way to view Glass House Poetry.
It's created from the Heart.

Smile for the World

Your Smile lights up the Room
Call the Fire Truck to put out the
Flame, no need for code red or blue.
Suspense is way too soon.
Race to the safety Net is your first clue.
Look, Listen and feel for a pulse.
Smile when you can see truth my love.
No need for a new Chapter.
Smile with the Dentist he's your biggest
Challenge. When he put on the finish touch.
You can look me in the eye again and smile
for the World. The code to every Heart is A
beautiful smile. No need to call emergency.
Smile my Love. Oh my Lord, I am healed.
Smile for the World release.

The Happy Clown

Where is my Costume
With the happy flame
Where is my Red Nose
Who knows my name
Where is all the fun
With the Birthday Cake
Where is the music, time
To dance with the happy
Clown. So many Baloons
To pass around. Commit
Your Heart to a Merry go round.
Get dizzy then fall down.
Open your eyes and embrace
All the colors, life is a Rainbow
forever, beautiful
When you celebrate every hour.
No time to frown, it's time to say
Cheese final memories with the
Happy Clown. Open your palm
and free me. On to my next Anniversary.
Happy, Happy Clown

Pink eye Monkey

Pink eye Monkey
Banana Trail under the
Golden Palm Tree.
Pink eye Monkey
Caption this Plush family
An open mind will gather
your thoughts, Pink eye
Monkey will eat freely.
Smile when you can see
yourself feeding a Nation of
pink eye Monkeys. Where every
Zoo is a stress release for families.
Always a big smile, when you read
Pink eye Monkey. Banana Dessert
For everyone who pet A pink eye Monkey.

Earth Angel Heart

The Heart of an Earth Angel is pure and True
Faith, Family and Friends are the solid glue.
Earth Angel shares in every Avenue
Community Love is a Corner Stone
Wellness is a promise. Hope is no mistake.
Peace is a silent Zone, we take when we meditate.
Earth Angel Heart is open wide to see the good in you.
Earth Angel is a Helping Hand when you're so cold.
Earth Angel is a Miracle, not code Blue.
Earth Angel Heart welcomes you.
In every challenge of life, Earth Angel knows that the
Code is love, like that white Memory from a Dove.
Send me a wing my dear.
Earth Angel have nothing to fear.
See yourself in the Heart of an Earth Angel.
Open to the tune of Love.

Pass me my costume
Paint on the fun
Send me some baloons
Tell me when it's done.
Remember my Red nose

My Fern Valley of Love

Today will come together for good
When I spend time in my Fern
Valley. Life looks brighter when the
Sun sheds some light on my Fern
Valley. Come out and share this
Peace of mind with me. This moment
Is meant to be free. Walk with your goal
In mind. This's for us. Everyone has a
Purpose, when you walk in my Fern Valley
With me. Escape, and enjoy this freedom of
Love. Butterflies everywhere in my Fern Valley of love.

Lily in my Garden

Beautiful Lilies from my Garden
Sending waves to my Brain.
White Doves flying around to
Sensor my love around the Lane.
Pink and Yellow Lilies just to
Name a few. Send me some
Roses to mix with thisView.
No need for a point of return.
Just an open mind willing to be
Creative and kind. Lily in my
Garden. Oops this bouquet is just
For you. Beautiful Green Lilies.
Your'e a chosen few.

Two Parakeets

Two Parakeets
A delightful part of Nature
Two Parakeets playing in
The water. Splashing and
sending Joy all over our minds.
Giving us Hope to unwind.
Grace and Faith live for a good
Laugh. Two Parakeets playing in
Their grass. Playing with theToys
that they bought for their Grandkids
Picking on the Food that they need
In order to live. Two Parakeets fun
in every sight. Two Parakeet in Broad
Daylight. Send in the Trees to welcome
Me. I am going to make friends with these
Two Parakeets.

Golden Clock Suspense

I love my Golden Clock
It can still tell the time.
I love my Golden Clock
Even though it needs extra
Time to unwind.
I need my Golden Clock
It makes me feel so fine
Sometimes I can hear a extra
Tick Tick Tock the sound from
My Golden Clock. I waited every
Hour just to feel the power
coming from my Golden Clock.
Now I feel so Relax free and unbox.
Smile and enjoy this Golden Clock.
Tick, Tick, Tock. Scrabble let's find
A tune for this Golden Clock.

A Good Laugh Daily

We need a Good Laugh Daily
We need to hear someone else's
Voice Daily. We Need a Fun Bed
Daily. We Need to Pray and Eat
Daily. We Need Activities Daily.
We need true Love Daily. Then our
Voice will escape and start enjoying
The Good Times Daily. We need Peace
Daily. Underline everything, but all we
Really need is a good Laugh Daily to clear
Our Lungs. Wellness forever Daily. Smile
There's Happiness for everyone. on a Daily
Note. Remember to always share a Good Laugh.

Life Golden Egg

Every time you read my Golden Egg
See a smile so bright.
Filter in your golden Keg
Memories and delight.

Take care of my Golden egg
Be the King and Queen that you are.
Cover every moment with a Star.
Smile when you share my Golden Egg
Every spark was meant to be.

Lavish yourself daily
Under this Palm Tree
Love and breathe openly
Search and find peace.

Everyone will see a Golden Egg someday
Compliment from the Ocean Breeze
Forever loved on every Anniversaries.
Life Golden Egg, one in every family
This poem was written by me.

Gifted Heart Future

Wrap this note in a box
Tie a ribbon that say affectionate
This is time sensitive, feel free to
Explore your mind with clean lenses
See from an open space
Gifted Hearts speak only of love.
Only time will see your embrace.
Gifted Hearts, Kisses for you
Teddy Bear mix with love Baloons
Gifted Heart everywhere is one clue.
Love without Judgment.
Stamp and save for Mr Rainy glee
Gifted Hearts on every Valentines Tree
Only love is welcome in this room.
Gifted Hearts happy Future with Balloons.

Cabbage From My Garden

Cabbage from my garden
Green, bold and Strong
Cabbage from my Garden
Help me to tag along
Be my crutch when I needed one.
sprinkle more water while I write
This excellent Poem
Cook me some Vitamin k and
Vitamin B6. Give me some fiber
and Potassium, World Healthiest.
Cabbage from my Garden looks very
Creative. Say no to Diabetes.
Enjoy Cabbage from my Garden
Wellness is no risk. It's for the best
One way to see Cabbage from my Garden.

Complicated and Fun Poem

You cannot Win for Loosing
You cannot loose if you Win
Smile and smell the Roses
Enjoy the line of a Gifted bling.
You cannot think without a
Thought in Mind. You cannot
Mine if you don't think.
Smile in every sitiuation
Life is a Genius Invisible Wall
When you can see me, go and
Give yourself a Wink.
Celebrate life, even if it's complicated
and fun. Center piece is only Love.

Memorial Garden Day

Flowers for my Memorial Garden
I want to see the Cross
Angels in my Memorial Garden
Memories that will last.
Butterflies in my Memorial Garden
Beautiful Birds too. Picture of my furry friend
Doggy pink shoe. Paint my Memorial Garden
Red white and Blue. Salute the Flag
That welcome me home for the truth.
Plant the word Love in my Memorial
Garden,please share with everyone.
Life is a bed of Roses, compliment from the
Sun. Memorial Garden Day will be open to
Every lonely Hearts. Forever Loved by a
Special one. Send in the white Dove.

Dress Like Money

Dress like money
Walk like money
Smile like money
Where is your funny honey
Wear the Dress that compliment your eyes
Wear the best suit to boost your V8 Engine
Talk like money, to open your Heart Rate
Think like money open the electric gate
Buy her the Monolo Shoes with the Rose on top
Someday this poem will clear you from any
Heart attack. When the passions of life come together
to give us a shock. Dress like money will be the center
piece. Everyone looking beautiful and free.
Make it rain with happy funny money.

Sitting by my Window

I can see and feel Happiness
When I Look outside my bedroom
Window. Beautiful flowers in my Garden.
Roses, Lily, blends with my Sunflower.
Daisy smiling with the Daffodils, oh how
I love every hour.
The Sun sparks my Joy, the birds play with
my favorite toy. Butterflies do bring me Hope
I find time explore and cope.
Every time I sat by my Window I feel so loved
Not Blue, Soon afterwards, The Rain will tell me
what to do. Remember the good times, now it's time
To enjoy the Rainbow. Nature visits me, every time I
Sit by my Window. Love is knocking at the door.
My Loyal doggy says beware. I will share you, no more.
Smiles kicks in. My Heart melts like a butter. Great dream
For the Future. I see Stars every Time I sits at my Window.
Open your eyes and say Gotcha. Now read this poem over.

Palm Tree Guru

Read me a Poem under the Palm Tree
Sing me a song under the same Palm Tree.
Meditate with me under the Palm Tree
Pray with me under the same Palm Tree
Love me Tenderly under the Palm Tree
Celebrate my Success under the same Palm Tree.
Feed me under the Palm Tree.
Shelter me under the same Palm Tree.
Lavish my thought with beautiful memories under
This Palm Tree. Guide me to a safe destination
When we leave this Palm Tree. It's fun to think deep
Talk to a Palm Tree Guru to master this field. Life is for
Keeps, Palm Tree Love just for you.

Every Beautiful Heart.

Every beautiful Heart
Comes with a smile.
Every open mind
Will find time to Unwind.
Every happy Hour
Will bring out good taste
Every Gifted Child is creative
Every Peace of Mind will not go
To waste. Every Challenge is a
Written test. Past around the Roses
Then share your Toys. Every Beautiful
Heart could enjoy a happy Clown.
Show the Golden box, then pass it around.
Take a gift, you're a beautiful Heart. We knew
This from the start.

Kisses Hiding Day

Kisses hiding in my Golden Egg.
Lipstick hiding under my Bed
It's fun to see your eyes wide open
Where are we going with this.
Give me an Idea to throw around
Give me an open space to take
On the Town.
Kisses Hiding in my closet,where is
My clothes. Chocolate Kisses base
With flowers. Where is my Golden shoe.
Make belief, everyone in the World
Have some form of Kisses Hiding for
Mr Rainy day. Oh how I love these
Kisses on payday. Dress like Money
Sees things one way. Show me your
Funny, Honey. Today is Kisses Hiding Day.
Who is wearing the Golden Shoe.

Raise Your Best Hand

I will Pray for the World
I will display Mercy
I will follow Gods command
I will search my Soul for the
Gala in your Band.
I will see your smile as a beautiful
Rainbow. I promise my right hand
To help you grow.
I will raise this Banner for a powerful
Glow. True love, true Hearts forever
Will flow. Raise your best hand and read
This poem again. One World with every
Dream on a Rainbow.
One Heart to put them together.
Raise your best hand for fun and say
Am-bi-dex-trous.

What If

What if the Plane crashes into the Moon
What if the Stars save the World for
dismissing this Idea way too soon.
What if the Human Mind has a missing
link from the beginning of time.
What if our memories resurfaces when we
See a Rainbow chime.
What if promises was a Policy to view.
Would you see Moon and Stars when you
See my clue. What if the Airplane is just an extra
Distraction, would you think different if I hold your hand.
What if all we need is an open mind, to unwind.
Just to relax and enjoy the difference in Mankind.

Golden Rose

This Golden Rose is different
This Golden Rose is spectacular
This Golden Rose will not quiver
This Golden Rose will be our focus
This Golden Rose will be around forever
Pass it around in the future.
The most important thing about this Golden Rose
It can see no color, the Base is a gloss.
This energy is love, the only way to see the Golden Rose
Explore and enjoy your Golden Rose today.
Someday everyone will own a Golden Rose to take away
Life Suspense. Golden Rose has a Sister Rose. She's
Golden too with something Blue.

Drawn To Numbers

Life is an open Book when you're drawn to Numbers.
One day we will smile and ask the Chef to come over.
Too many food for thoughts, too many mouth to feed
One day we will go in the Garden and pull up all the Weeds.
Life is a Jigsaw puzzle when you're drawn to Numbers.
Number 7 is my favorite, Someday I feel like a 10
Fun is a Mindset that can see what your'e thinking.
Crazy as it sounds, Life is anyone's guess when you're drawn
To numbers. Judge in your own space. Number 1 is waiting in
My space. Be creative when you're drawn to Numbers. Add
your
Number to mine. Someday this dream will come through.
Watch and read all your numbers in a Gallery of funny 2 shoes.

Maybe is no Doubt

Maybe I am from another Planet
Maybe I can see Mars from afar
Maybe Mercury is dangerous
Maybe Venus is about us
Maybe Neptune, Jupiter and Saturn
are all related. Maybe Uranus and
Planet Nine are in this Focus.
Maybe someday we will put things in
Order. Rearrange things and Enjoy the
Beauty of the Sun.
Maybe is no doubt, it's whatever you want
It to be. Free spirit on a Spree.

I Love The Sound Of Nature

I love the Sound of Nature
Can you see and feel the Raindrops
Bouncing off my Brain.
Can you see where your thoughts
Direct you to my Head.
Do you feel your Heart open wide
When the Sun showers us with
Vitamin D. Can you see everyone
Smiling, this notion is Mr feel free.
Indulge in the escape of Nature
Where every Golden Palm Tree
Will wave in the Wind.
Come to me my Love. I am the sound
Of Nature. The Moon and Stars will
Escort you home. In my Bed is a dozen
Red Roses, Enjoy the Silence, then open
Your eyes to the Sound of Nature. Outside
The Window is a White Dove to sing you a
Beautiful Song of Melody. Come to me my love
Lavish yourself with sound of Nature.

Poetry Under Wear

Poetry Panty
This one sounds Antsy
Smile in this moment
Might be a moment for
A wet stream.
Look around the Room
Could be a Merry go Round
Life is a ageing Machine.
Enjoy everyday like you don't care
Life is a Cool breeze when you read
My Poetry underwear. Two in one
World will someday wear my Poetry
Panty. Yay, thank you, thank you very
Much. Don't forget to wear this Golden color
Next time. Smile, everything is so clear
This moment belongs to the Poetry Under wear.

Golden Bra

I love my Golden Bra
It gives me support so far
I can live cool and free to tease.
Everything is Golden free breeze.
But my Golden Bra walks with my
Golden Underwear, Beware.
I even welcome my Golden shoe.
I feel so pretty, I might wear my Golden
Dress, this's a test. Every Golden Bra
Is special, with no worries in the World.
Just a Handsome guy to give me a Twirl.
Oh how I love your Golden Bra.
Let's read this poem again.
This time around send the Models in.
Dance and jump out of your skin.
Right now I am seeing everything Golden.
Start with the Golden Bra.

Jamaicans Dance under the Coconut Tree

Americans Dance under the Palm Tree
Crazy fun on every Anniversary.
Expand your thoughts to see me.
Plug in your Mellow Mood and see Bob Marley
Light us the Ball Room and see Elvis Presley
Legends forever will be apart of our Party
Life is a circle. Go around for Honor and Brave
Don't forget the Maroon Slaves.
Every Country have Tester, That's why we will
Always remember our Ancestors.
Jamaicans Dance under their Coconut Tree
Americans Sings under their Palm Tree.
Look deep. we're one Family Circle.
It's fun to be Nutty, and Pretty funny.

Paulette Lewis-Brown

Ants Nest Dilemma

I just want to kick away the Ants Nest from
Under your feet.
I just want to keep you safe from any retreat
I just want the Bite to be even
In this world, Ants Nest show up in every season.
Cultivate your Grass, keep it clean from toxicity
Watch the beautiful flowers welcome me.
I just want to kick away the Ants Nest from under
Your Feet you see.
Honesty is always a good Medicine.
Let's celebrate and be Merry.
No more Ants Nest in this Vicinity.
Free to Love freely.
Don't quiver, This's the Ants Nest Dilemma.

Guess Today's Color

In the Palm of my Hand is
Today's color. In your Brain
You will find the correct answer.
If you need a clue
Think of A Rainbow shoe
Blend with the Sun for more fun.
Dance in the Rain for a gifted blessing
Guess today's Color and be the
Winner of my poem clue.
Oh how I love America and Jamaica too.
Smile to this one, and wave with the fun.
Now open your Palm.
Someone now own today's Color forever.

A True Friend

A true Friend
Will be a Rock
Someone to Cry to
With Sugar on top
Someone to Love
Without Judgement.
Lighten every doubt
Then share Flowers
Stand in every Crises
Then pull down the prayers
When I think about a True friend.
It's Gods greatest Blessings.
Forever Bonded for life.

The Golden Deer

Nature sends the Deer my way
In my Backyard with a shade of grey
So many Deer under the Trees
Look at their perky eyes looking at me.
This's so beautiful, Lord I feel so free.
Seven Golden Deer enjoying life's beauty
With me. Light a Candle and celebrate this
Dream with me, on every Anniversary.
Your Gift is A Golden Deer.

Golden Angel

On Top of the World
You will find a Golden Angel
Praying.
On top of the World you will find
A Golden Angel Meditating for
Peace.
On top of the World you will find
A Golden Angel Loving in every
Aspect of life.
Living freely in a Bed of Roses.
Reading and sharing Love from
A pedestal of freedom.
On top of the

My Golden Turtle

I love my Golden Turtle
Someday it might box me in.
Corner me and put me in a SHELL.
I love my Golden Turtle with my slow
self my Mind will collapse and my Turtle
will enter in. Now I can see my Golden
Turtle with big eyes and his underwater wings.
Escaping slowing is my Turtle in his Golden Shell
Free me from my Master, free me from my mistress.
I want to be in the Wild with my other Turtle family Tree.
I need to eat Fishes, drink Water, Walk in the sand.
Where are the Earthworms to play along.
Smile and say, where is my Golden Turtle.
To sing me a Golden Song. Snap, Snap is the sound
Of my Golden Turtle.

My Golden Thorn

Feel free to hold my Golden Thorn.
It will not cause any distress
Feel free to touch my Golden Thorn
It will not bite you or harm you.
This Golden Thorn will be a positive
Force with a momentum of clues.
Peace and Love will carry us through.
My Golden Thorn will not be a burden
A very powerful Gift will be attached to
This Golden Thorn. If you can find it.
Keep it for a read over. Wear this Golden
Thorn with Grace and Freedom of speech.

Nature Under The Sea

let's walk on the Beach
Show me the Ocean Glory
Wrap your Arms around me
Send my Heart into a frenzy.
Think of everything beautiful
Show me Nature Under the Sea.
Feel Adventurous and free.
Enjoy the cool Breeze every
Anniversary. My mind always
Wonders to Nature Under the Sea.
Fish me your line, every time you
Can see me. Swim your thoughts over
Here and rescue me. Your'e my Nature
Under the Sea. Forever you will be the
only one for me. My Golden Palm Tree.

True Friend

A true friend is one of life's greatest
Blessings.
A true friend will stay with you to the end.
A true friend will help you around the bend.
Helping and Caring all wrapped up in love.
Great Attributes of True friends.
Take a true friend on this Journey
Share this Gift, great memories forever.
True friends. loved by all.
Enjoying life under the Star.
Drinking Lemonade and Red Wine
Everyone having a fun time.
Cheers to our True Friends.
Forever Bonded.

I Love My Husband/Wife

Love your Soul Mate
Love your Name sake
Love the one that knows
When your sick.
Love everyone in life, but
Don't forget to love your
Husband or Wife.
Heavenly Bond that no one
Can break. Genuine love to
Give and Take.
Forgiveness is at every Gate.
Pray Daily and learn to continue
with your welcome Plate.
Husband and Wife on every Base.
One God to watch over us.
No Judgement, just Love your other
Half everyday and be blessed in Grace
Forever.

What if everything was Golden

Golden Families
Painting in a Golden House
Golden Garden under a golden Cloud
Golden Palm Trees everywhere
Golden Showers many to spare
Golden Ideas from every corner
Golden Cars to escort the Winner
Challenge me to a Golden Art
Nature my Avenue with all the Golden
Stars. Everything Golden is your Theme.
Golden in a frame of Masterpiece.
Put your Golden in my Golden Basket
Send the Golden dog and the Golden Cat
To reveal this Gift. Everything Golden.
Enjoy this Golden Smile, with this Golden
Poem. Gold and Bold to Win.

Jesus is behind every Scene

Gossip all you want about me.
Jesus is behind every scene.
Laugh all you want behind my back
Jesus is behind every Scene.
Lie and believe your lies about me.
Jesus is behind every Scene.
The beauty of this is, I am Jesus beauty
Poetry Queen. Believing in myself is all
I need. Because Jesus is behind every Scene
To tell me everything. So feel free when you're
Working behind the scene.

I am a happy Bunny

I am a happy Bunny
You might find this funny.
Happy, happy, Joy, Joy
Oh how I feel to highlight that.
Honey mixed with my Golden Carrot.
Send me some Vegetable and
Fruits, fresh water and my Miracle
Pill cute. Green grass my entire Avenue.
I feel like a happy Bunny still in pink and blue.
Fill up my cup, let it overflow with Joy.
I am a Happy Bunny with a lots of Toys.
Repeat after me. Happy, Happy Joy, Joy.
I am a Happy Bunny Jumping for Joy.

2019 Super Bowl

I love to enter a Zone that no one dare to enter.
I love to score from an Angle no one saw coming.
Genius invisible wall was my first Chapter.
I love to see your face when your read my Journey.
I hope to travel in every Quarter without a gurney
North, South,East and West one way to see the World.
However this World is a Two way stream.
Stay focus on Tom Brady, don't leave out the Cooks.
Life is still a Eagle everyone knows how to hunt food.
MVP could be anyone best count.
Everyone is a winner and a Star on the Golden field.
Love is still in everyone back pocket. Hungry for this win is
Worth the Ticket. My Score for the 2019 Super Bowl is 32-27
This could be fun if everyone learn to create Wings. Not
everyone
Will make perfect sense. That's why Jesus gave me a call every
time.
He wants to see a Poem on #Super #Bowl. Explore in my World.
Only Winners will Win. Make it Rain, Green and smiles
Everywhere.
Save me a Chicken Wing with a glass of Lemonade. Fun to get
your
Attention in 2019 under this Golden Palm Tree.

Share With The World

Give without Mercy.
Love unconditionally
Find peace within
Learn how to Swim.
Float for the moment
I am watching over you.
Angel on Earth is your first
Clue. Give freely it's attached
to your Heart. Your Soul will never
Be forgotten . Your Books will last
A lifetime.
Share with the World. This Poem
Is from a Guardian Angel.

Someday

Someday I will be a Golden Palm Tree.
Give me my space and my Privacy.
Don't try to cloud my Mind with your new
Ideas. I live my life under the Shelter of
Peace and Love. Now my Roots are dried up.
Yet I am still alive to be me. Free from any
Controversy. Someday I will be in Heaven
With the other Angels enjoying Super with
My true friend. Someday the World will learn
To find daily passion in themselves. Smiling
Everywhere will be Faith, Family and Friends.
Feel Free,to Visit when Possible. I am now a
Golden Palm Tree. Praying and waving daily.

90 DAYS DRILL

I survived your Ninety day drill
Not because I am the weakest Link.
But because I am the strongest to think.
I observe fake and real struggle to be real.
Then I observe Bully and Instigator work it out.
I smile from a distance with my EMT knowledge.
Then I focus on my Mentor in Heaven who sends
To College. I live to learn in every circumstances.
North, South, East and west. My Job is to always
Be a Helping hand. Provide for the people in need.
I never worry about fake friends, because in Reality
Jesus is really my Best friend. I survive your 90 DAYS
DRILL because it was in his Will. Learn to love everyone
With and open mind. Plots and scheme doesn't work every
time.
On any Team. Give freely with no Judgement. World needs
Peace.

Winner and A Star

Two people to sit beside me.
My way of saying, think freely.
Your'e a Winner.
Your'e A Star.
Both will share this space in good
Grace.
One will Hope for a surprise.
The other will be playing with Choice.
Two future Gifts could be yours to keep.
In this World life should be very Sweet.
Wrapped up in Nature of true Love.
Golden Palm Tree could turn into a Turtle Dove.
Smile with your many clues. Name the Gift for
Today. It will be yours to keep. Have Fun, Stay
Happy and Sweet.

Transformer for Jesus

Stop My Poems Are Talking.
Look at Me. I Am now
The Walking Poet's Tree.
Enjoying two Countries
So I wrote JAmerican Poetry.
Feel free to Test your Heart
I am the Author of Poetry Pacemaker
Sometimes I feel like an Earth Angel
So God sends me Dreams from beyond the skies.
In this World, it's all about our Loving call.
See why I wrote Genius Invisible Wall.
This Poem will be given for Free.
I am now the Golden Palm Tree.
This's about Us, Transformer for Jesus.
Give Praises to him.

The Golden Money Store

Amscot, the Golden Money Store.
No judgment loan given to the poor.
Big or Small everyone is welcome.
Amscot will make your Tootsie Roll.
Smile and enjoy Amscot Money Store.
Money, Money Galore. Best Customer
Service for sure. That's WHY I selected Amscot
as the Golden Money Store. Heads up to
Education plan. Give this Golden Store the first hand.
Money, Money, for the Poor.

Our Fathers Closet.

I started this Journey many years ago.
I leave my children to carry on the flow.
I gave my all to the poor.
With open arms I always open my door.
Now I am in Heaven watching it grow.
All my Friends and Family show.
With Tears of Joy and Grace inside.
I am please to say, God Bless Our Fathers
Closet. Faith will always be our shoulder of rest.
Peace and Love to Our Fathers Closet.

Happy Golden Birthday

You are one Year Older
Set your Goal.
Enjoy from every Corner Stone.
Ocean and the Sky will be Super
Large enough to call the Birds
And Trees. Nature everywhere is
your first Choice. Family and
True Friends will be standing by.
This's your day for a Fun glide light.
Gifts everywhere, Love in every corner
To share. Smiles, from Heaven is coming
Through, Now it's time to sing Happy
Happy Birthday to you.
It's great to feel Golden too.
Happy Birthday to you.

Golden Chocolate

If I was a Golden Chocolate
I would feed the World daily with
Love. I would enter your life twice
On Birthdays and Anniversaries just
To charge your Heart with laughter.
If I was a Golden Chocolate I would invite
Golden Roses to come over. Sunflower and
Lily peeping through the window. Golden Chocolate
Will welcome smiles from every head quarter.
Gifts at arms reach, say out loud Black Chocolate is good
Forr the Heart and the dancing feet. Oh life would be so sweet
Only if I was a Golden Chocolate. Family and Friends delight
Would be a caption of me. Golden Chocolate Spree.

Hospice for our Furry Friends.

Loyalty dances and wiggle their Tails
Their time is coming to an End.
We should care. The pain will be hard to
Bear. We will carry memories in our mental
Block, we would watch the time on our Golden
Clock. One day our Furry friend will be going
To Doggy Heaven. Give them a good life on Earth
Their love and Loyalty will always be remembered.
Hold their Paws and Tickle their Ears. Life is never
The end when we lost our Furry Friends. Pray and
Welcome Hospice for our Furry Friends.
Forever Bonded in comfort.

Hide Behind Jesus Love.

Hide behind Jesus in Difficult times
He will carry you .
Hide behind Jesus in fun time.
He will celebrate with you.
Hide behind Jesus
Follow in his footsteps
He's the only perfect one.
Hide behind Jesus
Pray and Meditate Daily
Jesus knows your burden.
When you gets weak
He will carry you.
Hide behind Jesus
He always know your Location.
Someday he will give you Wings.
To Celebrate with friends.
Hide behind Jesus my Love.

There's No perfect Family.

Every Family will face Struggles
It could be the Economy or Health reasons.
Remember that Prayer is the number one care
Medicine. Faith will be your recharge Battery.
Peace will be your mindset to confront every Test.
Hope will someday be by your side. Grace and
Your furry friends will be at your bedside. There's no
Perfect family, so forgive everyone. Enjoy life journey
With your favorite song. On my last breath read me a
Poem. Jesus is my Best Friend. He's waiting to welcome
Me home. Forgiveness is on every door. Ask and he will
Come in for sure. Don't fool yourself. In this World there's
No perfect Family, Amen Just feel like a free comfort
Breeze. That's welcome by every Family Tree.

Education is the most powerful Gift to give.
Share wisely. The Young Minds look up to
their Mentors. RIP Dr Lionel V Mangue.
Poetry is everything even in a Dream

Carry on with the Golden Palm Trees. In Memory of everyone who died of Cancer and Heart Diseases. Enjoy life, give it your best.

Printed in the United States
By Bookmasters